PORTLAND TRAIL BLAZERS

RICHARD RAMBECK

COVER AND TITLE PAGE PHOTOS BY MATT MAHURIN

Published by Creative Education, Inc.

123 S. Broad Street, Mankato, Minnesota 56001 USA

Art Director, Rita Marshall
Cover and title page photography by Matt Mahurin
Book design by Rita Marshall

Photos by: Allsport; Mel Bailey; Bettmann Archive; Brian Drake; Duomo; Focus On Sports; FPG; South Florida Images Inc.; Spectra-Action; Sportschrome; Sports Photo Masters, Inc.; SportsLight: Brian Drake, Long Photography; Wide World Photos.

Library of Congress Cataloging-in-Publication Data

Rambeck, Richard.

　Portland Trail Blazers / Richard Rambeck.

　Summary: A history of the Portland basketball team whose name reflects the history of its home area.

　ISBN 0-88682-518-0

　1. Portland Trail Blazers (Basketball team)—History—Juvenile literature.　[1. Portland Trail Blazers (Basketball team)—History.　2. Basketball—History.]
I. Title.

GV885.52.P67R36　1992　　　　　　　　92-204

796.323'64'0979549—dc20　　　　　　　　CIP

PORTLAND: HOME OF THE TRAIL BLAZERS

Almost 200 years ago, American explorers Meriwether Lewis and William Clark blazed a trail across the United States to the Pacific Northwest. Lewis and Clark's epic journey opened up the area for American pioneers. In 1845 some of these pioneers set up a trading post at the point where the Columbia and Willamette rivers meet, and the city of Portland was born.

Portland has since grown into the second-largest metropolis in the Pacific Northwest, with a population of more than 400,000. Its location between two major rivers makes it one of the busiest port cities on the West Coast.

Portland owes much of its success to the courage of trail-blazing pioneers such as Lewis and Clark. So when the

Trail Blazer great Geoff Petrie.

Future Blazers coach Rick Adelman was named the team's first captain.

National Basketball Association (NBA) granted Portland a franchise in 1970, the club's owners decided to call the team the Trail Blazers. At first, not too many fans followed the trail to the Portland Memorial Coliseum to see the expansion franchise. Only about half of the arena's 12,000 seats were filled that first season. Within five years, however, it became almost impossible to find a ticket to watch Portland's only professional sports team. In fact, the Trail Blazers have had nothing but sellouts since the mid-1970s.

EARLY STRUGGLES AND A TOWERING NEW STAR

Like most new NBA teams, the Trail Blazers struggled in their first few seasons. Portland fans, however, did have a pair of outstanding players to cheer for—sharpshooting guard Geoff Petrie and versatile forward Sidney Wicks. Petrie, a graduate of Princeton, was Portland's first pick in the franchise's first draft. He came to Portland with a reputation as a shooter, and he lived up to his advance billing by scoring more than 40 points in a game 10 times during his six-year career with the Trail Blazers.

Wicks joined the team the year after Petrie did, coming from the University of California at Los Angeles. At UCLA, Wicks had led the Bruins to national championships in 1969 and 1970. He was big enough to play center and quick enough to be a small forward. For Portland, Wicks proved to be Mister Everything, as he made the NBA All-Star team four times.

Wicks and Petrie gave the Portland fans plenty of thrills, but they couldn't lead the team to winning seasons or to the playoffs. After the 1973-74 season, in fact, the Trail Blazers had the worst record in the NBA's Western Conference.

Mister Everything, Sidney Wicks.

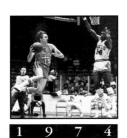

Larry Steele lived up to his name, leading the league in steals with 217 for the season.

That earned them the right to the first pick in the 1974 draft, and there was no doubt which college star the Blazers would take. His name was Bill Walton, and like Sidney Wicks, he had been a leader on college championship teams at UCLA.

Actually, Walton was more than a star at UCLA. He was considered the best center to play college basketball since another UCLA legend, Kareem Abdul-Jabbar. Walton's UCLA teams were so good they didn't lose a game during his sophomore and junior years and won the national championship both seasons. When Walton's college career ended, all the experts said he was the type of player who could turn any pro franchise around. What none of the experts could have predicted, though, was how injury-prone Walton would be.

When the Trail Blazers drafted Walton, their fans started dreaming of an NBA title. Most of these fans had watched Walton during his college career when he played against the University of Oregon and Oregon State University. During Walton's rookie season with Portland, the fans—and the experts — expected Walton to do for Portland what Abdul-Jabbar had done for the Milwaukee Bucks. They expected him to make a bad team into a very good one right away.

THE RAMSAY SYSTEM SUCCEEDS

During Bill Walton's first two pro seasons in Portland, the redheaded center didn't transform the Trail Blazers into an NBA contender. He didn't have the opportunity, because he had more injuries than great games. Portland coach Lenny Wilkens got fired because he couldn't make the Blazers winners. But Wilkens didn't have a healthy Bill

Walton. The next Portland coach, Jack Ramsay, would succeed, in large part, because Walton stayed relatively injury-free for a while.

Ramsay came to the Blazers in 1976 after leading the Buffalo Braves to the playoffs three straight years. "Believe me, Jack Ramsay's performance in Buffalo was no accident," said Portland executive vice president Harry Glickman. "Jack possesses one of the best minds in the game, and he's a brilliant teacher and motivator."

Ramsay also had a new Portland team to work with. Wicks and Petrie had been traded. Maurice Lucas, a muscle-bound power forward with a frightening glare, replaced Wicks in the starting lineup. The guards were steady Dave Twardzik and spectacular Lionel Hollins. The small forward was Bobby Gross, a smart player who hardly ever made a mistake. The center was a new player, too. It was a healthy Bill Walton, who proved to be just the kind of player Ramsay could build a team around.

The Portland coach was known for his colorful, almost wild, wardrobe, but his philosophy of basketball was simple and direct. Ramsay preached discipline and the need to control the pace of the game. This was done with an aggressive defense and a controlled fast break. Ramsay required his players to be well-conditioned so that they could beat their opponents up and down the court.

Ramsay's system wasn't designed to produce stars, only victories. He demanded unselfishness, and he got it, especially from Walton. The big redhead loved to pass and control the offense. Walton, considered by some experts to be the best passing center in the history of the game, ignited the Blazers' fast break with his outlet tosses off the defensive boards. He keyed the half-court attack with laser-

1 9 7 5

Sidney Wicks pulled down 27 rebounds in a game against the Lakers, setting an all-time Portland record.

Lionel Hollins energized a new Portland backcourt.

Power forward Maurice Lucas.

First-year guard Lionel Hollins was named to the NBA All-Rookie team.

beam passes from the high post.

Walton was finally living up to his potential, mainly because he had no major injuries to contend with. "I'm just healthy," Walton explained during the season. "For two years, I wasn't able to run up and down the court freely without making a conscious effort out of it. Without thinking about it. That's no way to play basketball. I love this game. I always have, and I always knew how good I was."

The rest of the NBA was also finding out how good Walton could be when he was healthy. "The guy just keeps storming at you," said Phoenix center Alvan Adams. "They should win the division easy."

The Blazers didn't win the Western Division in 1976-77, but they ended up winning much more. Portland beat Chicago and Denver in the playoffs, and then faced the Los Angeles Lakers in the Western Conference championship series. It was Walton against Kareem Abdul-Jabbar, one great UCLA center against another. It was no contest. The Blazers ripped the Lakers in four straight games as Walton dominated Abdul-Jabbar.

Portland had earned the right to play the powerful Philadelphia 76ers in the NBA finals. Philadelphia stars Julius "Dr. J" Erving and George McGinnis led the 76ers to victories in the first two games. But something happened late in game two. Maurice Lucas and Philadelphia center Darryl Dawkins had a brief but spectacular fight. Dawkins had tried to intimidate Lucas, and "Big Mo" showed he wouldn't back down. It proved to be the turning point of the series.

The aroused Blazers won three straight games, giving them a chance to wrap up the series at home. Although Julius Erving scored 40 points in game six and did everything he could to prevent the Blazers from winning the title, Walton and his teammates were too much for the rest of the 76ers. The Blazers broke out to a 12-point lead with less than five minutes to play. Then they withstood a furious Philadelphia rally that cut the lead to 109-107 with only 18 seconds left to play. That was just enough time for one last bit of heroics from Bill Walton. As the clock ticked off the final seconds, McGinnis drove to the basket, but Walton rejected his shot and sent it sailing all the way to midcourt. In the meantime, the horn sounded, and Portland fans raced onto the floor to celebrate an NBA title.

The next day 50,000 people lined the streets of downtown Portland for a victory parade. The fans came to cheer the best team in the NBA—and one of the youngest. Walton, who was named Most Valuable Player of the playoffs, had completed just his third year in the league, and

1 9 7 7

Bill Walton led the NBA in both rebounding and shot-blocking.

most of the other players were in their mid-twenties. Gleeful "Blazermaniacs" predicted the team would win several titles before Walton finally retired.

1 9 7 8

Powerful forward Maurice Lucas was named to the NBA All-Defensive first team.

A SHORT-LIVED DYNASTY

Blazer fans' predictions of a Portland dynasty looked pretty accurate midway through the following season. The Blazers raced to a 40-8 record, and were 50-10 when Walton's injury woes returned. His feet hurt, and he missed several games. Portland struggled in the last two months of the regular season, but still finished with a mark of 58-24, the best in the league.

When the playoffs began, the experts said Portland was the team to beat—but only if Bill Walton, who was named MVP of the league, was healthy. In Portland's first playoff series against Seattle, Walton started at center in the first two games. The surprising SuperSonics won the first game in Portland, but the Blazers came back to take game two. Unfortunately, the victory came at a huge price. Walton went down with an ankle injury and did not return during the series. X-rays showed that he had a broken bone in his foot; soon after, the Blazers and their fans faced broken dreams. Seattle defeated the defending NBA champs in six games.

The Blazermaniacs were shocked, but they were even more upset months later when Walton announced that he wanted to be traded. Walton told the Blazers that his injuries had not been treated properly by the team's medical staff. Portland eventually granted Walton his wish, sending him to the San Diego Clippers for several players and draft choices. It was a sad day in Portland when the big redhead

All-time great Bill Walton.

Lloyd Neal became the first Blazers player to have his uniform number (36) retired.

left. Even sadder for NBA fans was that constant foot problems prevented Walton from ever being a full-time star again.

REBUILDING WITH VANDEWEGHE AND DREXLER

In order to become a championship team once more, Portland had to rebuild. Coach Jack Ramsay developed quality clubs around center Mychal Thompson, forward Calvin Natt, and guard Jim Paxson. But the Trail Blazers couldn't seem to make it past the second round of the playoffs.

Before the start of the 1984-85 season, the Blazers made

High-scoring guard Jim Paxson.

Portland had high hopes for Sam Bowie.

*Mychal Thompson
led Portland in
rebounding for the
fourth straight year.*

two important moves. They traded Calvin Natt, center
Wayne Cooper, and guard Lafayette Lever to Denver for
high-scoring forward Kiki Vandeweghe. Then the club used
the second pick in the 1984 draft to take Sam Bowie, a
7-foot-1 center from the University of Kentucky. Portland
hoped to build another championship team around a
mobile, versatile center, which they believed Bowie was. In
drafting Bowie, the Blazers allowed the Chicago Bulls to
take a guard from North Carolina with the third pick. That
player's name was Michael Jordan.

In retrospect, the Blazers may have made a mistake in
passing up Jordan for Bowie, but the club's officials knew
they already had a player whose skills were similar to
Jordan's. In the 1983 draft Portland had used its first pick to
take Clyde Drexler, a high-scoring, high-leaping guard from
the University of Houston. Drafting Jordan wouldn't

have solved Portland's biggest problem: the lack of a dominating center.

Ramsay had hoped to build a team around Bowie on the inside and Vandeweghe on the outside. But Bowie spent most of the time on the sidelines with a cast on his leg, and Vandeweghe had trouble adjusting to Ramsay's system.

After Portland lost to Denver in the first round of the 1986 playoffs, Ramsay was replaced as coach by Mike Schuler. The following season, the Blazers won nine more games than they had the previous year, and Schuler was named NBA Coach of the Year. The main reason for the improvement was Vandeweghe, who had become one of the most feared scorers in the league.

Kiki Vandeweghe set new club records for points scored (2,122) and scoring average (26.9).

"Obviously, most of the guys I play against are more talented than I am," he said modestly. "I have to outthink them, and I have to work a little harder. That's all that made me whatever I am today, practice."

Vandeweghe would wait for a defender to do something wrong and then take advantage of it. "He [the defender] is always going to make a mistake—leaning the wrong way, too close, the wrong foot forward, shifting his eyes," he said. "You just have to wait for his mistake and capitalize on it."

Vandeweghe's best weapon was his jump shot, although he really never jumped that much. "The higher the jump," Vandeweghe explained, "the more inconsistent the shot is. The real good shooters in the NBA...don't jump real high." Vandeweghe also had a quick first step that allowed him to drive past defenders who got too close. "The only person who can stop Kiki," said Los Angeles Clippers scout Kevin O'Connor, "is Kiki."

Led by Vandeweghe and Drexler, the Blazers were the

Clyde the Glyde.

highest-scoring team in the league during the 1986-87 season, averaging nearly 118 points a game. Portland was even better the following year, finishing with a 53-29 record. Vandeweghe had another good year, but it was his best friend, Drexler, who really dazzled Portland's opponents. "The fans are only now coming to realize the kind of player we have in Clyde," Schuler said.

CLYDE GLIDES TO STARDOM

Clyde Drexler had come to Portland with a reputation as a great leaper who had average shooting, ball-handling, and passing abilities. He also was considered only an average defender. But Drexler, who is known as "Clyde the Glyde" because of his smooth moves on the court and his ability to leap higher than much taller opponents, soon showed he could do it all. Drexler was chosen to play in the NBA All-Star Game practically every year. He also became the most important player on the Portland team. "Clyde's our man, no question about it," said Portland point guard Terry Porter. "He doesn't have to be our go-to guy, but we need him to make the big plays."

But Drexler's critics—who included Portland coach Mike Schuler—believed Drexler wasn't enough of a leader. "I think I have been a leader by example, every year," Drexler argued. "I think I am a guy who knows how to win."

The Blazers, however, didn't know how to win in the postseason, losing in the first round of the 1987-88 playoffs. A year later the team's record fell to 39-43, and Portland lost again in the first round of the playoffs.

1 9 8 8

Jim Paxson became the first player to score 10,000 points as a Trail Blazer.

Left to right: Kermit Washington, Buck Williams, Jerome Kersey, Cliff Robinson.

A NEW COACH AND NEW STARS

As a result of the Blazers' playoff losses, Mike Schuler lost his job. The new coach was Rick Adelman, a former Trail Blazer guard. Adelman told the players to relax, to stop trying so hard. He knew that young players such as Jerome Kersey, Terry Porter, and Kevin Duckworth needed confidence, not pressure. Adelman knew the talent was there. It just had to flow freely.

Clyde Drexler scored 30 or more points in 25 games during the season.

The Blazers' new young stars had been discovered in the most unlikely places. Duckworth, who played in college at unheralded Eastern Illinois, came in a trade from San Antonio. Porter was a standout at Wisconsin–Stevens Point, an NCAA Division II school. And Kersey played at tiny Longwood College near Washington, D.C. He came to the Blazers as a raw talent with great athletic ability and an intense desire to succeed. At first Kersey was known only for his dunking, but he soon became an excellent scorer and rebounder.

Kersey and Duckworth matured and improved dramatically during the 1989-90 season, mainly because of the presence of power forward Buck Williams. Williams, who came from the New Jersey Nets in a trade for Sam Bowie before the season began, brought the mental toughness the Blazers needed to become a great team. He never slowed down or failed to go after a rebound or loose ball. He ended up leading the team in rebounding.

While Williams helped turn Portland's frontcourt players into a winning combination, it was guard Terry Porter who was mainly responsible for leading the Blazers to a 59-23 record in 1989-90. The bull-like point guard was the guy who ran the show, the one who kept Portland from becom-

The Blazers present a formidable lineup (pages 26-27).

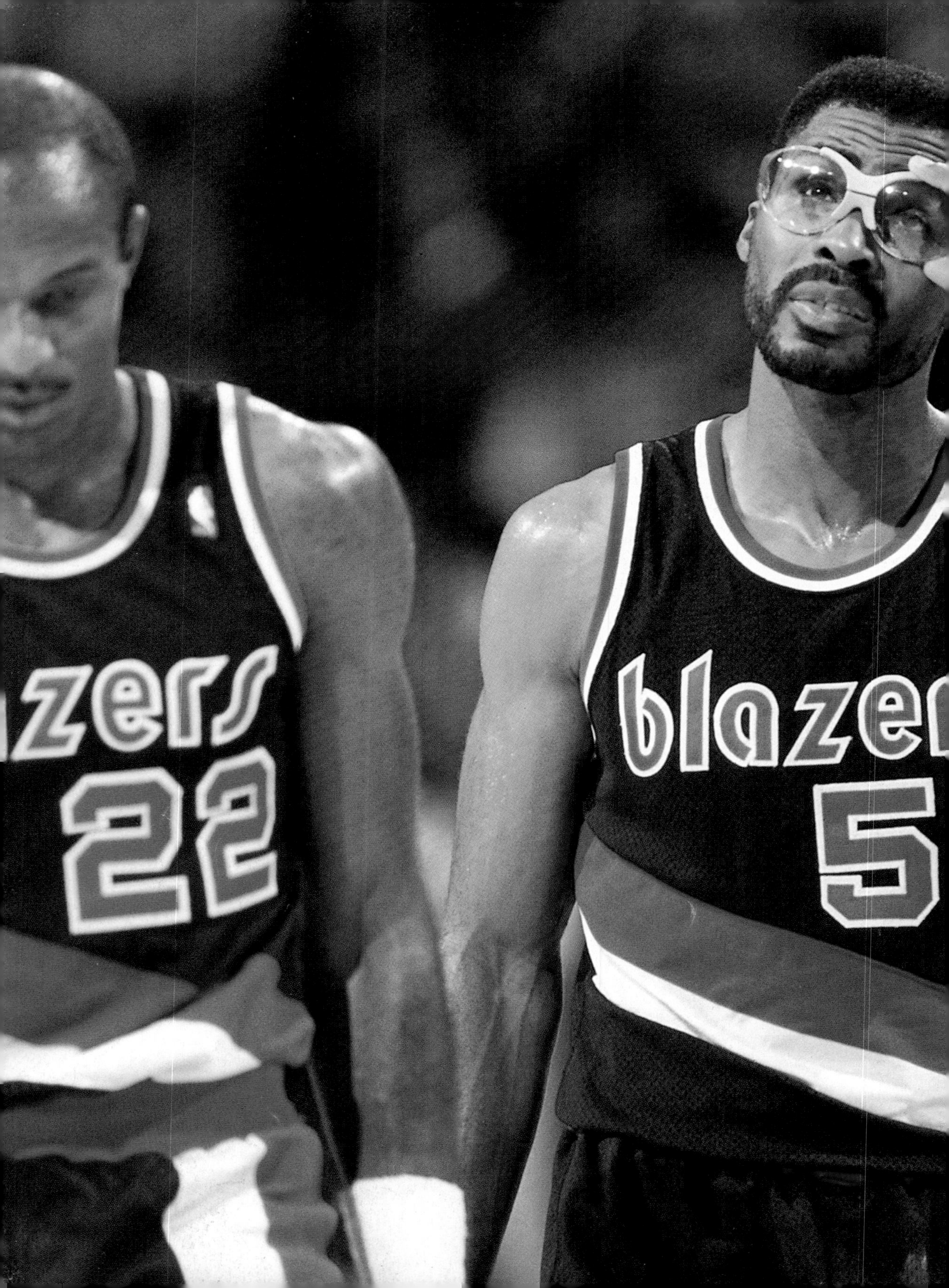
zers
22
blazer
5

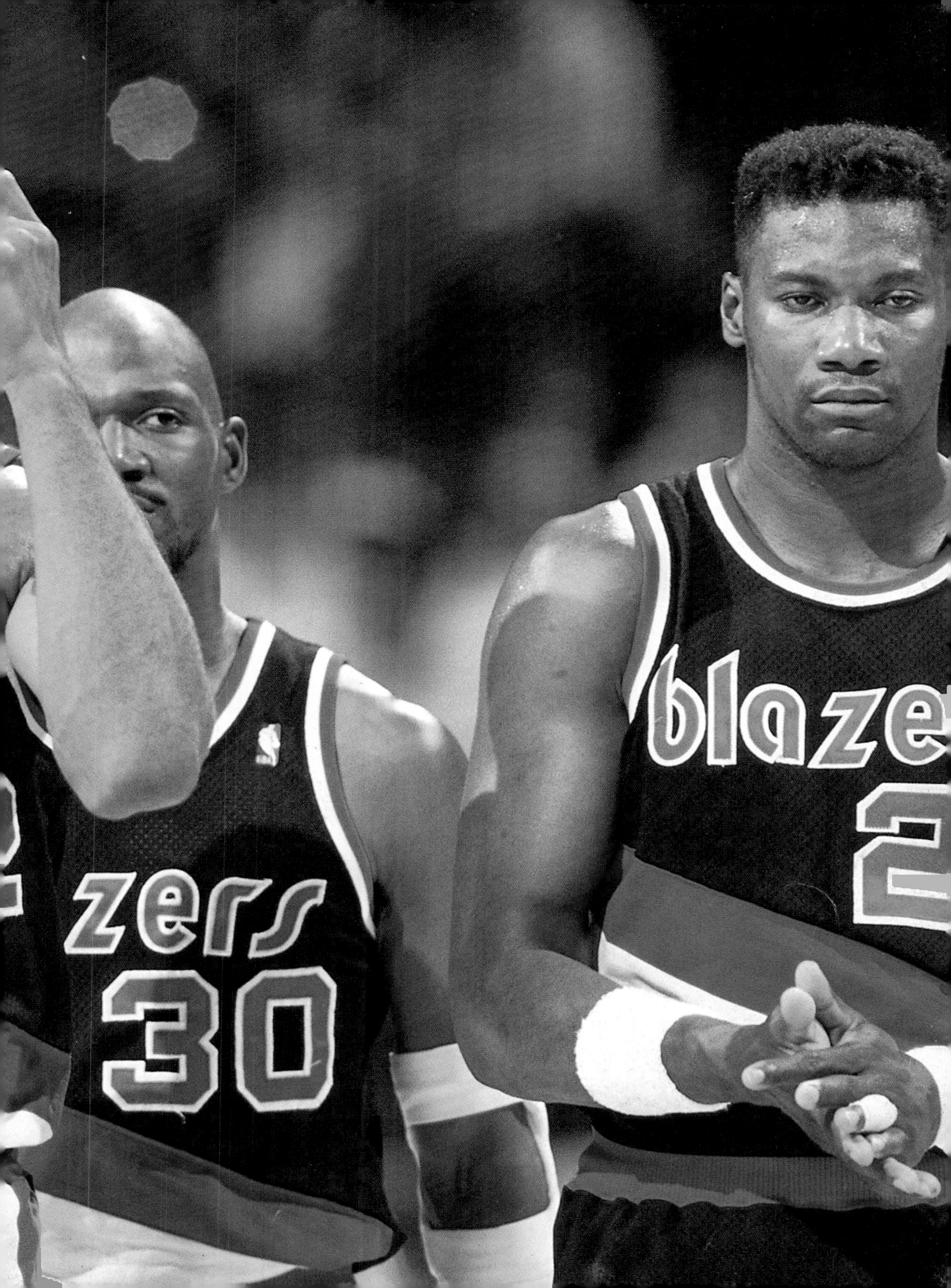
zers
30
blaze
2

For the third season in a row, Terry Porter averaged more than nine assists per game.

ing a selfish team. Players such as Drexler, Kersey, and Williams got most of the credit, but Porter was the key. "Like any good underrated player," wrote David A. Raskin of *Sport* magazine, "he battles without flash and razzle-dazzle. When the game is on the line, the ball usually ends up in his trusty hands—not Drexler's—for the big shot."

Porter proved his value in the Western Conference finals against Phoenix. Portland won game one, but trailed 106-103 in the second game with time running out. Then Porter took over. With Phoenix point guard Kevin Johnson draped all over him, Porter buried a three-point shot to tie the game. The crowd at Portland Memorial Coliseum went wild as Phoenix failed to score on its trip down court. When Portland regained possession, Porter drove toward the hoop, jumped...and swished a 10-footer with 13 seconds left. The Blazers won 108-106. "We should have won the ball game—I don't mind saying that," said Phoenix coach Cotton Fitzsimmons. "Porter stuck it in our face."

Porter and the Blazers beat Phoenix in six games. Portland then advanced to the NBA title series against the defending league champion Detroit Pistons. The Blazers played the Pistons tough, but in the fifth and final game of a tight series, Detroit guard Vinnie Johnson ruined Portland's hopes of victory. He hit a 15-foot jumper with less than a second to play, giving the Pistons the win.

LOOKING TO THE FUTURE

The Blazers came close to winning another championship in the 1990 playoffs, and they vowed to win it all the following season. Trades brought veteran guards Danny Ainge and Walter Davis to Portland. Both were

1 9 9 1

Buck Williams was named to the NBA's All-Defensive team for the second straight year.

excellent shooters, something the team-oriented Blazers needed in clutch situations. Portland won its first 11 games and 19 of its first 20 games in 1990-91. Porter, Drexler, and Jerome Kersey all had great years as the Blazers posted a 63-19 record, the best mark in the league that season and also one of the top ten records in league history. Their fine playing enabled the Blazers to win the Pacific Division for only the second time in team history.

Portland vied against the Los Angeles Lakers in the Western Conference finals of the playoffs. The Lakers held a three-games-to-two lead going into the sixth game of the series, which was played in Los Angeles. The Blazers fell behind, but battled back to within a point with time running out. Portland worked the ball around for a potential game-winning shot. Suddenly Porter saw an opening, drove toward the basket, and let fly with a jumper. It was the type

The athletic Terry Porter.

Blazer center Kevin Duckworth.

of clutch shot he had been making all year. But this one rimmed out. Magic Johnson grabbed the rebound, and Portland's season was over.

After the game a disappointed Clyde Drexler shook his head. "We just didn't have it in this series," he said. "We're a better team than we showed. We'll be back."

There's no reason to doubt Drexler's prediction. The Blazers are still a young team, a team with a tremendous amount of talent. In fact, many experts believe the current Portland club has more natural ability than the Bill Walton gang that won the NBA title. But the Walton-led Blazers have something the present team members don't possess— NBA championship rings. Portland fans are hoping that situation changes soon.